THE CRY FOR FREEDOM

THE CRY FOR FREEDOM

THE STORY OF A PORN ADDICT

ELISHA KOLADE

The Cry for Freedom: The Story of a Porn Addict
Copyright © 2014 by Elisha Kolade

Published in United Kingdom
by EKM Publications

All Rights Reserved.
No part of this publication may be reproduced, stored in a retrieval system, or transmitted, in any form or by any means–electronic, mechanical, photocopying, recording, or otherwise without prior written permission.

For information:
177 Charles Street, Stonecrossing, Kent,
DA9 9AL, England.

Print ISBN: 978-0-9929320-1-5
Ebook ISBN: 978-0-9929320-2-2

Cover design by Imaginovation Ltd.

Interior layout by Maureen Cutajar
www.gopublished.com

I dedicate this book to my wife, Temitope, who faithfully supports me in everything I do.
I love you with all my heart. You are a special blessing.

All my love,
Elisha (Ty)

CONTENTS

1. YOUNG AND CURIOUS 1
2. MY SECRET BEST FRIEND 13
3. MY VERY FIRST ENCOUNTER WITH SEX 23
4. WORLD WIDE WEB PORN 29
5. THE MAN WITHOUT A BRAIN 37
6. OVERPOWERING DESIRE 43
7. LIVING ON THE STREET 49
8. SOMEBODY CALL THE AMBULANCE 53
9. IS THIS STD?!!! 59
10. I AM BROKE 63
11. WHY THE GUILT? 65
12. THE CRY FOR FREEDOM 75
13. FIRST NIGHT WITHOUT PORN OR MASTURBATING 81
14. WILL I SURVIVE? 85
15. WILL I EVER GET MARRIED? 93
16. CONGRATULATIONS! YOU MADE IT 97
17. YOU CAN BE FREE 99

1

YOUNG AND CURIOUS

There are three ways a child will be educated about sex: the parent, the media or the internet. The choice is yours.

"What is a young boy like you doing in front of the mirror every morning before heading to school? I have always said, if you impregnate any lady... I promise you will be solely responsible for the upbringing and responsibility of both the lady and the child. It seems to me you are more concerned about your looks rather than your academics." Mum gives me that stern warning look and turns to leave.

Why is mum always going on about the same thing over and over again? Doesn't she get tired saying the same thing every day? I wish she could just stop. I am sick and tired of hearing her going on about me impregnating a lady, day in day out.

Hear mum going on about me impregnating a lady when she knows very little about me. I was very sure she hadn't a clue what her boy was up to each night as she slept in her room nearby. Not even my immediate younger brother knew what his big brother was up to while he was fast asleep in the same room. My other brother was way too young to know what I was doing for him to report me to my parents. My sister had moved into her own room so she didn't have a clue either. Everyone was oblivious. I occupied and dominated my own world without any interference from any of them.

Mum rarely visited my room. She controlled the entire house straight from the kitchen with her powerful voice while baking her pastries for business. Whenever she came in to check my room, all she ever did was to stand at the door and take a quick glance just to ensure the bed is laid, shoes are in the right place, and there are no clothes on the floor – typical of many African mums. If the room was in a mess, she would just give you that quick piercing look with pursed lips and you'd know what would follow if her instruction isn't carried out promptly and precisely.

Dad never came into my room either but unlike mum who said the same thing over and over again, he never really said much. All he would do is make a comment or two about what he needed you to do. If that task isn't completed, what follows is not a discussion but a well-aimed smack. I had studied both of them long enough to know that all I had to do to keep them away from my room was simply to ensure the room was kept tidy.

School was more fun than being at home especially during break times when the 'Genesis', my group of close friends met. I wasn't initially part of the Genesis. It was made up of seven young, cocky guys and I was always counted as the 'sub', meaning that I wasn't really part of the founding members of the group. I was an add-on, a sub-ordinate. To me it didn't really matter; as long as I was with my group, nothing else mattered.

My group had a code of conduct that required you to have money, attend house parties, look nice and wear branded perfume at all times – yes, that was it for us 12 and 13 year olds! Whatever the case, I ensured I never missed the school playground for anything. If I missed the playground, then I missed out on the latest news about who is dating who, what teacher is being picked on and every piece of gossip there was to guzzle. I sometimes looked for ways to come to school over the weekend. This always sparked my mum's interest in knowing what we would be doing at the weekend that couldn't be completed during the week. As always, her usual line would be, "I need to know your friend; don't you have friends in school? Ehn?" There I was thinking to myself, *why will I want to you to know my friends mum?* I had to cunningly wriggle myself away from her interrogation, eventually escaping exhausted from her questioning but gleeful at the prospect of a fun day ahead with the Genesis group.

WHAT IS SEX?
Over time, the group had developed various signals that we used to communicate even while the teacher was teaching. Every eye movement meant something; every finger or leg movement was always saying something. While we

might not be talking to each other during lectures, we were constantly communicating with different signals.

Everyday my friend, G and I always had our lunch together before joining the rest of the group. On this particular day, the bell rang as normal. I signalled to G, but it seemed he wasn't interested. That caught me by surprise. I approached his desk to ask if everything was alright. His reply was simply, "I am fine! ". Within the Genesis, I was closest to G than the rest of the boys. I knew when something was bothering him or if he was trying to hide something from me, but he kept saying everything was fine.

"What about the guys? Are we meeting at the usual location?" I asked. He mumbled some words about them meeting somewhere. I thought to myself maybe he wanted to be left alone. I decided I would go by myself and try to find out from the rest of the group if they had any clue as to what might be wrong with G.

The group were nowhere to be found. Then, I remembered G saying they were meeting somewhere. As I headed back toward the class trying to figure out what was going on, I saw my group sitting together in a circle. As soon as I called out, they quickly stood up and acted as if nothing was happening. I asked why they had decided not to meet at the usual place without letting me know.

"Oh! Ty, sorry for that?"

"So what are you guys looking at?" I asked.

"Nothing, we are just having the usual chat." Gab replied.

I knew there was something wrong from their shifty behaviour but really couldn't work it out. I explained that G was alone in the class and was not interested in coming out? They just laughed it off, leaving me baffled.

The next day, the same thing happened again. G wasn't interested in hanging out. I also noticed there were boys that weren't normally part of the group joining them. As soon as they saw me coming, they stood up acting as if nothing was going on. I was really confused. *What is happening? Why was everyone talking in hushed voices?* I said to myself there must be something they were either discussing or doing that they really didn't want me to know about.

With time, I was becoming disinterested in school. I felt alone; the playground was not as fun as it normally was. It seemed my group was leaving me out of the group. Each time they saw me coming, they acted cold towards me. G wasn't as friendly as he used to be and nobody was saying anything. G and I only spoke briefly and even so, he wouldn't discuss what the other boys were discussing.

School seemed very boring. I began toying with the thought of not going to school anymore. The challenge though, was I couldn't tell my parents why because I knew for a fact that my mum would want to know. Knowing my mum, she would follow me to school to ask my teacher what had been happening to her boy. That would've made things even worse.

One day while sitting alone having my lunch, G walked over to where I was sitting and sat at the table next to mine. What a surprise!

"Is there any problem? Why aren't you with the rest of the group?" I asked trying to hide my relief and excitement.

He smiled. I knew G very well. He had this mischievous

smile that was always loaded with more than words could say. "G, what do you want? Why aren't you with the group?" He smiled still staring at me.

"Ty! Would you like to know why the guys are leaving you out of their discussions?"

My eyes lit up. I dropped my snacks straight back into my lunch pack. "Of course I want to know," I replied.

He looked around the classroom cautiously to ensure there was no one listening to our conversation. He leaned towards me with his eyes still darting around watchfully and said, "SEX". I opened my mouth to shout but he quickly placed his hand over my mouth trapping my words in their cage.

"Shush, Ty! You've got to be quiet about this or else you will get me into trouble."

"Sex! What is it about sex that you guys are discussing that you do not want me to know about?"

"They believe you do not know anything about sex," G replied still looking around nervously.

"Is that what they are discussing each time they are sitting in a circle and when they see me coming, they quickly scatter like a bunch of bees?"

"Do you want to know what they are doing when sitting in circle?"

"Yes I would like to know."

"Sex magazine!"

"Sex magazine? What is sex magazine, G? What is inside?" I asked. Just as G was about to mention what was in the magazine, the bell rang for the next lecture. He got up. I got up too but reluctantly. I needed an answer.

Arriving back home from school that very day, I headed towards my room without stopping to see what was for lunch. I just wanted to be left alone. Opening the door to my room, I saw both of my younger brothers jumping on my bed. "Get down from my bed," I yelled at them.

"What is your problem? This room belongs to me as well and I can do whatever I like," replied my younger brother.

After a while, my younger brothers left the room and I was alone. Immediately, my thoughts switched to what G had said in class about not knowing anything about sex. *Is it true what G said about me not knowing anything about sex? Who do I ask? I dare not ask my parents what sex is.* I could just imagine what mum will say or do. I know for a fact she will say, "I am coming with you to school tomorrow. I want to know who has been teaching my boy about sex." She would properly ask me why I wanted to know about sex. "Do you want to know how to impregnate a lady?" she would then say as she normally does every morning before I leave the house for school. "If you impregnate any lady you will be the one to take care of both the child and mother".

Who else could I speak to about sex? Should I ask dad about it? I doubt that dad would not discuss it with mum. I wished I could ask him but we were not that close. *Who could I ask what sex is? Should I approach my teacher and ask? What would they say? Would they be able to help or would they laugh about it? Who then could I ask?* There I was, lying on the bed deep in thought. It had been four hours since I got back from school when my mum's piercing voice broke my concentration. "Why haven't you eaten your afternoon food?" mum asked.

"I am not hungry, mum."

"If you know you are not eating what I cooked for you, can you please go and put it inside the fridge. Please, don't waste food and make sure you have completed your night chores before you sleep".

Getting to school the next day, I couldn't wait for break time to ask G if he himself knew anything about sex. Immediately the bell rang and Miss P declared break time, I was running towards G. Getting to his desk, I applied my brakes, pulled out a chair and sat next to him.

"Ty, why are you running?" G asked.

"Do you know about sex yourself?" I replied.

"Ty, do you want to have lunch or do you want to discuss sex".

"Both" I replied. G then started laughing.

"Why the laughing, G"? What is sex if you know about it?"

I noticed he wasn't ready to talk. "If you would not tell, I am going to ask the teacher!" I said. Then he began to laugh even more for about three minutes. I was irritated.

"G, could you just answer my questions and stop laughing" I said.

"If I knew the answer to your question, Ty, do you think I would not tell you?" G replied. "Do you think I know anything about sex? All I have seen so far, for the first time myself, is the magazine being passed around and the DVD the guys have been watching."

"What DVD?" I asked.

"There is a DVD that is being passed around which the guys are talking about."

"G, do you know my mum is always going on about me not impregnating a lady." G stood up and began to laugh even more. "What is so funny about that, G?"

"What is funny, Ty, is your mum going on about you impregnating a lady. That is funny, Ty. How could your mum say such a thing to you? I am going to help you with your question if you promise you would not tell anyone what am about to tell you." I promised him nothing we discussed would ever get out. This was an exciting development. At last, I would come to the end of my predicament!

G continued, "If this goes out, it will be the end of our relationship. So you must be really sure before you answer. Not even your parents could know about it. Do you understand, Ty?" I could see he was serious.

"I do understand, G Could you go ahead and say what you need to say please?"

"Within the group, everyone is taking turns to watch the sex DVD. Next week, it will be my turn to take it home to watch. If you are interested, you can come along over the weekend to watch it too."

"Of course!" I replied, excitement welling up in my belly. "I will like to see the movie." By then I couldn't contain my happiness; I was so ecstatic.

The day couldn't have come any sooner after the day G spoke to me about the sex DVD. The thought of seeing the movie was too much for me to contain. I was constantly thinking about it. I would soon be able to know what sex is all about! G and I agreed to watch the movie when his parents were out at the weekend. I told my mum I would be going to G's for the weekend. She was okay with this, and of course, as always she had to remind me to complete the house chores before leaving. That was her tool for managing me.

On the day I was to meet up with G, I got up very early in the morning to ensure I completed my chores so mum wouldn't stop me from going. Throughout the day, I put on my best behaviour just to ensure nothing would stop my plan for the day. On arriving at G's house, his parents and siblings were all out. So, we had the entire house to ourselves.

Just as I was about to jump on the couch, G said, "Ty are you ready to watch porn?" He caught me by surprise. porn?

"What is porn?" I asked. "I thought we agreed we will be watching sex movie. So what is it you are calling porn?" As always G started laughing. "What is so funny, G?"

"There is no difference between porn and sex," he replied. "They are both the same thing."

"Are you sure, G? Because I thought we are watching sex movie. I am kind of confused."

"Shut up and watch. You are asking too many questions," G snapped.

He had exposed my naivety but I was ready to shut up. My long-suffering was about to yield dividends. As he was about to insert the sex DVD, my heart started pounding. I could sense my body shaking. Sensing my anticipation, G said, "Relax, Ty! It is only just a movie; there is nothing to be shaking about."

Wow, what is this I am seeing? Is this the sex thing my friends were always discussing in school or what? But, G just called it porn. Hundreds of questions began to flood my mind right where I was seated. *What is porn? Is porn sex? Is sex porn? Why are the man and woman screaming?* I had no clue about what they were doing.

My mind was racing so fast it seemed I would explode. G called it porn and at the same time called it sex. I didn't know which of the two was correct but this man and woman in the movie looked as if they were having so much fun whatever they were doing. All through the movie, I began to think to myself if any of my friends in school had tried the stuff I was seeing on TV. *Could they have?* If they have then I need to get hold of this movie too and watch it all over again. All these questions were on my mind when I realised the movie had just concluded. Right!

As soon as the movie finished, I knew something had broken loose within me. Lots of questions that needed answers were racing through my mind. *What were they doing? It seemed they were enjoying themselves.* Right there, I asked G if he could lend me the movie he called porn, but his reply an emphatic no!

"What must I do in order to see the movie again?" I asked.

"I have to return it back. If you are interested in seeing it again, you will have to ask Gab next week at school".

The week could not have come sooner. Arriving at school without any hesitation, I headed towards Gab's class.

"You okay Ty? Why does it look like you are about to beat someone up?" Gab said.

"I want to see the sex movie," I replied with a firm tone.

"What sex DVD, are you talking about Ty?" I wasn't fooled by the feigned expression of innocence.

"The porn movie," I reacted

"What porn movie?" Was he having a laugh? Well, I wasn't having it. So, I said, "Don't mess me about, Gab. All I need to know is when I can borrow the movie."

"Okay Ty," Gab replied dryly. "You will get your turn but you have to abide by the code of not sharing it with anyone, or else you would not like what would happen to you. If it does happen, it's from your end the movie gets lost. Then you are out of the group."

He was only 5 feet 3 inches tall. I normally call him the loner. He never laughs much and his eyes were always red. Everyone in the group feared him because although he never talked that much, he had fearsome bloodshot eyes.

"No problem I will make sure it is not lost I will keep it," I promised.

I was part of the group again! I was now on a desperate quest to know what the man and woman were screaming about. I just had to get my hands on the sex DVD.

The week that followed was such a great one for me because of my 12th birthday. But, most especially because it was my turn to take the sex movie home. I was so thrilled; I felt I was walking on the clouds.

2

MY SECRET BEST FRIEND

Your imagination is the engine room where both your present and future are created.

"Ty, do you know you could get magazines that look like porn?" G said.

"Are there porn magazines?" I asked.

"Ty! Why do you always act as if you don't know anything?"

Looking around cautiously, he pulled me aside and handed me magazines just outside the school gate. Straightaway, the magazines dropped to the floor. As soon as I saw what was on the front cover, G quickly picked it up and held my shoulder tight.

"Ty what is wrong with you? Do you know you could get me into trouble with your naivety? What if someone had seen the magazine?" I could sense he was irritated and nervous.

"I am sorry, G." My hand was still shaking from seeing what was on the front cover. "What is porn magazine, G? Is it the same as porn movie or sex movie?" There were so many questions going through my mind that needed answering. *Could there also be porn magazine? Is it different from the movie I saw at G's place? What could be inside this magazine?*

"Ty, you are asking too many questions. Will you like to have your own copy or not?" G asked with obvious irritation in his voice.

I didn't hesitate; I just said, "Of course, I will like to have my own copy but how can I get one? Can I borrow yours?"

"No, you cannot borrow mine Ty. You will have to buy."

"Buy?! How could I buy one when I have no money and where do I know such a magazine is sold? How can I afford it, G?"

"Take it from your mum's purse," was his casual reply.

"Are you stupid?! What if I get caught? No, G, I would not do it. I would not steal from my mum."

"Then you can't have the magazine and I can't borrow you mine either."

Back home I could not help but think about what G had said. *Should I ask mum for money? She will ask what I need the money for. But, what if I steal and I get caught? I'd definitely be punished. But, I need to get the magazine and G's advice seemed the best option for me.* After much consideration, I decided to follow G's advice. I decided to wait till mum went into the shower because that was the only time I could have access to her purse.

As soon as mum was in the shower, singing like she always does when having her bath, I stepped into her room. I was so shaky as I looked around to ensure both my brothers and my sister were somewhere else playing. Immediately I stepped into mum's room, I went through her purse. The plan was that if I heard any footsteps I would hide under the bed. I went through mum's purse, got some money and ran out as fast as I could, my heart pounding in tune with my steps.

Next morning at school, I shouted from the top of my voice, "G, got it!" He signalled back. I shouted back but I couldn't read his lips to understand what he was saying. Without thinking about whether other students might be listening, I yelled, "The money," at the top of my voice. He looked around and quickly nodded his head meaning 'cool'.

On our way home, we stopped in front of a corner store just as we planned in school earlier.

"Ty, this is the store I spoke to you about. When we get inside, I will do the talking. You just watch and listen," G said. As soon as we stepped into the store it seemed G and the store owner were the best of friends.

"Hello, G! How are you doing? I haven't seen you this week. Where have you been?"

"I have been very busy with school work," G replied. "Meet my friend. His name is Ty."

"Hello Ty! How are you doing?" The store owner said as he turned towards me.

"I'm very good, sir," I replied trying to hide my obvious discomfort.

"How can I help you guys today?"

"Both I and my friend would like to buy a sex magazine," G replied. I almost died. "What is wrong with you, Ty? Why are you stepping on my toes?"

"Why do you have to tell the store owner we are both

here to buy sex magazines," I whispered to him still reeling in my embarrassment.

"Do you want the magazine or not?"

"Yes, I want the magazine," I replied.

"Then, let me do the talking and you just watch?'

"Okay."

The store owner noticing things suddenly weren't right asked whether we were okay.

"We are okay sir,! We were just having a quick chat" G quickly answered with a feigned smile.

"You know where the magazines are located, G. Let me know if you require my help."

The store owner could definitely sense I was shy. He pointed in the direction where the magazines were displayed. G pulled my shirt while I followed behind him.

"Are you okay, Ty? It seems you are going to faint?" G asked.

My body was shaking profusely. It seemed my heart would stop at any moment. My legs were so weak. I thought I might pass out.

"Ty, are you sure you are okay? Would you like to go outside and get some fresh air" G asked. "I am okay, G" I replied.

The shock of seeing naked women right in front of me on a magazine cover was too much for me to comprehend. I couldn't believe what I was seeing. It was like the very first day I saw the porn movie at G's house. Just like that day, my heart was beating so fast. I felt I would pass out right there and then.

"Happy now ?" G asked.

"Yes. I am."

"Be very careful where you keep it. Make sure you keep it where your mum will not see it."

"Of course, I am not that stupid"

Normally, I would drop my bag on the couch and that is where it will be till our private lesson teacher arrived. But, as soon as I got home, I headed towards my room. Mum's shrill voice followed me as I bounded up the stairs. "Are you not hungry?" she asked. "It is not like you to be going straight into your room."

"I am fine, mum," I replied but she wouldn't let go.

"How was school?"

"School was fine. I just need to drop my bag."

"That is good for a change," she said falling for my excuse.

I nodded while I walked to my room. Making sure nobody was coming into my room, I quickly hid the magazine under my bed. I ensured I didn't leave my bag around like I used to. This time I carefully tucked it somewhere underneath my bed. While I was eating, my thoughts were on the magazine. I could not wait for the night time to arrive. As the night was drawing closer, I began to get tense.

"When are you going to bed?" I asked my brother.

"When did you start getting interested in when I am going to bed?" my brother retorted.

"I am just asking. I will be going early."

"That is strange? Are you sure you are okay," my brother asked.

"I am okay," I replied casually. I knew that if I decided to go to bed early he would definitely follow me and he did.

Once in the room, I acted as if I was sleeping. Not very long after, I heard my brother snoring. I stood up, gently shook him slightly to ensure he was fast asleep. I walked towards the door to ensure everyone was asleep. As soon as I realised they had all gone to bed, I switched on the light and started looking through the magazine. It was only when I heard footsteps that I realised it was 3 am because that was the time mum usually woke up to start baking for her business. Quickly, I ran to switch off the light and jumped back into my bed. But, I couldn't sleep; there were so many mixed emotions; the joy of having my own sex magazine and not being caught by my mum was overwhelming. I couldn't wait to see it the next day. From that night onwards, I began waking up to look at sex magazines.

As time went by, I was spending more time in the room looking at them alone. My parents were never suspicious of what I was doing alone and I also ensured my tracks were well covered. My mum still went on about me impregnating someone at school, and she still did not know what I was doing while she slept. But, her words were the least of my worries. My collection of sex magazines was swiftly growing. My lunch money plus all the money I stole from my mum's purse was now going towards funding my collection of porn magazines. But, my greatest concern was storage. Underneath my bed was now full. I needed another place to keep my treasured stash. My only option was keeping it with friends.

Over time, I realised I could close my eyes and act as if I was having sex with the ladies in the porn magazine without having to touch them physically. I was ecstatic when I discovered I didn't have to ask a lady for sex. I discovered I could have sex with any of the ladies in my school without even asking them for sex just by imagining it my head. *This is a cool discovery*, I said to myself. *No one can tell me what to do and what not to do with any lady; I can control everything by myself now!*

After I had begun to use my imagination to have sex with ladies in the porn magazines, I realised something was wrong. Each night, I had pain in my private part after looking through those magazines. I began to have the urge to act out what I had been seeing in the porn magazines and porn movies; but, it seemed mum's warning about impregnating a girl was my biggest problem. Those words wouldn't just leave my head.

Now, my parents did not even disturb me whenever I was in the room alone. My mum would nag about me being in the room alone while the family was spending time together. I always just ignored her. Like every other day when I was alone in my room, I would just be going through the sex magazines thinking and acting out whatever I saw on the pages. One day, while thinking and acting as if I was sleeping with a lady I liked in the magazine, I felt a sticky liquid on my hand. I ran to the toilet not drawing any attention to myself and quickly locked the door behind me. I could not understand what it was, but right there I was relaxed and at the same time scared. *How did this happen?* I remembered I had been unconsciously rubbing my private part while thinking about sex and doing what the guy was doing to the lady in the porn magazines. *Should I tell G what was happening to me? Will he know what it was?* I decided I was going discuss it with G because the guys in the group might know about it.

One day at school, my friends and I were discussing the different kinds of porn movies we had seen so far, when somebody mentioned the word masturbating. "I know masturbating," G said and he went on to explain what it was – it was simply what I had experienced that night. I decided I was not going to tell anyone because of the way they were laughing about people who masturbate. "People that masturbate are not doing the real thing," G said. Within myself I said, "Wow! There was no way I was going to discuss it with any of my friends."

As time went by, I began to masturbate every day. It developed into my daily routine. Soon I began to wake up very tired from staying up at night. Waking me up to go to school was becoming a challenge for my mum who still didn't know what I was doing. Sometimes, while she was working in the kitchen at about 3 am, I was still awake going through my magazines.

I began to see my porn magazines as the only thing no one can deprive me of, a world where I could do whatever I liked. I began to use porn to encourage myself when things were not going the way they should either at home or school. Whenever things were not going so well between my mum and I – like when I'm punished for not doing or completing a task, I would console myself with my porn magazines. When I was deprived of going out, I would tell myself that there is one thing no one could take from me, and that is my porn magazines. The night season became the only time I looked forward to every day. I became more joyful when everyone had gone to bed, because the night time was my time where I could do whatever I liked in my own world.

Turning 16, I knew masturbating wasn't good enough for me any longer. I needed to try out the real sex. I told myself, *I have got to practice what I have been seeing in the porn movie. I had to experience it at all cost.* Having discovered masturbating, I knew it allowed me to act as the man in the magazine with the woman; but, I knew there was more. From then on, I began to think of ways I could have sex with a lady. *Should I ask my girlfriend in school? She would probably laugh at me. What then are my options?*

3

MY VERY FIRST ENCOUNTER WITH SEX

Sex is free but only in the context of marriage

It was summer! The sun was out in full. No more school and assignments. Now was the time to enjoy the holiday. Every holiday, the Genesis regularly threw different house parties. This season was no exception. 'Who is dating who?' and 'Who is sleeping with who?' were always discussion topics each time the group met. Some days, the guys would be hanging about whispering to girls or teasing them as they walked past.

When there is a talk about sex and the best position, everyone knew I would make the most noise about what I thought. What my friends didn't know was that I had never had sex with anyone before. Whenever there was talk about whom my girlfriend might be and if I had ever had sex with her, my reply was always the same. "Guys, I am not going to discuss what I am doing with my girlfriend." I was clever enough to ensure there wasn't inkling.

"Ty, are you sure you have ever had sex before?" G' asked.

"Yes, of course," I would reply ensuring I sounded irritated by the question. But, it was a lie. These lies I had kept solely to myself knowing deep down inside me that I wanted to attempt what I had been imagining every night.

Everyone particularly liked going to G's house simply because he lived in a beautiful part of the town. His house was always packed throughout holiday. On one of those lovely summer days, I was with the Genesis guys at G's house. We were doing the usual – having fun and chatting about women.

"Ty, we're heading out will you like to come along?" G asks me.

"Yes I replied".

In the cab I asked where we were going.

"You ask too many questions, Ty! Why can't you just wait until we get there and then you can decide for yourself if you like it or not. And, if you don't, you can leave!" Lee replied. The other guys grunted in agreement.

"Guys, I don't think there is any crime in asking where we are going. Anyways, I'm not paying for the cab!" I replied.

As we approached a T-junction, G told the cab driver to drop us there and asked us to get out of the cab. No one seemed to know where we were apart from G and so everyone was asking him where we were.

"Come off?" I said. "We are in the middle of nowhere." I surveyed this strange environment.

"Don't worry, Ty. We're not going to kill you," one of the guys said as the others laughed and mocked my uneasiness.

"If this is a joke, I will not appreciate it, guys," I said.

"Guys! Relax. Why are you acting like a bunch of kids? Where we're going is just a walking distance," said G, as he confidently began strutting along the road towards this mystery place.

By then, I was becoming really scared especially as everywhere was dark. There were no street lights and to me, we were in the middle of nowhere. *Who will find me if something terrible happened to me?* I began to panic but no one could see how terrified I really was because it was pitch dark and hardly could I see my steps.

After walking for about four minutes, we started hearing music coming in our direction. As we got closer the music got louder.

"Where is this place G?" I asked.

"Relax, Ty. You will thank me later when you find out." G replied. He definitely shared none of my fears. He was just calm.

"Really, what will happen if something bad happens?" G ignored me and continued going with the guys in tow.

About ten meters from the gate, the music was even louder. My first shock was the number of cars parked outside the building and the level of noise coming from the house. In fact, it was booming, blasting and you could hear excited voices as if there was a party. Just as I was thinking about that, G stopped and turned. "Guys, do you know where we are?"

"No," replied everyone except Lee, who by now was laughing profusely. I was right. Lee knew where we were coming.

"Welcome to the home of prostitutes."

"Prostitutes? Who are they?" I was puzzled. Again my naive mind was introduced to another alien word: prostitutes.

"Ty, prostitutes are people you pay to have sex with."

"Pay? Why do I have to pay to have sex with a lady?" I replied.

"Ty, you pay because sex isn't free," Lee replied with obvious irritation as if it was something that I really should have known. *Prostitutes? Pay to have sex?* I just didn't get it.

"I don't think I have got the money to pay for sex," I replied.

Still irritated and getting impatient, Lee replied, "I will lend you as long you pay me back." I promised to pay him back and he fished around in his wallet for some cash and shoved it into my hand.

"In that house, you can have as many ladies as you want! The world is in your hand. Have fun guys!" G said that with so much glee and I received it with just as much anxiety and perplexity. *Pay for sex?*

"Have fun? What fun is there in having to pay for sex," I asked.

As we approached the building, we came across numerous men pouring out of it. "Where are all these men coming out from?" I asked. "Ty, you are asking too many questions," replied Lee.

Just as we entered the building, we were met by men with bottles of beer in their hands. They were chatting heartily and joking but I could not sense what there was to joke about in this wild house. I quickly switched my attention towards the lady that was staring in my direction.

MY VERY FIRST ENCOUNTER WITH SEX

Inside, the building was dimly lit but I could not miss the rows of women wearing nothing but bras and mini-skirts staring directly at me just as we walked past. I could smell the strong odour of alcohol; so strong that I could hardly breathe.

Something that struck me most was that these girls looked just like the ones in the porn movies and porn magazines. Just as I was clearing my throat, one of the ladies grabbed my hand and whispered into my ears. "I am yours for tonight" She then pulled me towards her room. I was following and wondering whether the lady knew I had never had sex before. *What am I going to do?* "What is your name, young man?" she purred as she looks straight into my eyes.

"My name is Ty!" At that point, my heart was pounding. I was alone and the guys hadn't prepared me for any of this.

"How many hours will you like to spend with me?" she asked. She was stretched out on the bed undressed and asking me to bed.

"Hours" My eyes and mouth widened with disbelief. *Hours? Hours having sex?*

"It seems you haven't done this before"

"I haven't!" There was no point lying, was there?

"You will be fine. But you will have to pay first!" She smiled as she asked me to pay her first.

"How does it work?"

"It's by round, young man. Every time you come inside of me is one round. Do you understand?"

I did. With the money Lee lent me, I made a payment for one round. When we finished she asked, "Did you enjoy yourself!"

"Yes! It wasn't bad." I replied.

"I hope I will be seeing you again young man." she said.

She was right! After that night, I knew all I needed was money and I could have sex whenever I wanted with any prostitute. All I needed was money. I didn't need to pressurise my girlfriend for sex; she probably would never know what I had been doing behind her back. This was the beginning of countless visits to prostitutes over the next 14 years.

4

WORLD WIDE WEB PORN

*It takes only a click to open a porn site
and a few visits to get addicted.*
Lois Tverberg

My college result wasn't the best, but I got the minimum pass mark required to get me into my chosen university to study computer science.

"On behalf of our vice chancellor, we would like to welcome our entire first year students to LU University. We hope you find your next three or four years exciting. As you go around the campus, you will come across students wearing a red vest that reads, 'Can I help?' Please feel free to ask them any questions and for directions if you find yourself lost. Once again we would like to wish you all the best of times as you join us in building your career."

As a computer science student, most of my time was divided between attending lectures and practical exercises in the laboratory. The laboratory was an open space with hundreds of computers that anyone could use. One day, I was in the laboratory for a practical software programming lesson. As I was settling in, I noticed there were a couple of boys sitting next to where I was setting up. They were discussing the latest movies and which ones were the best of all time. "Godfather! Godfather is the best movie ever made," I said.

"And you are?" One of the guys in the group asked. All eyes were on me now.

"Ty, I am a first year student," I replied.

"Well, Ty, you can join the discussion if you are interested. My name is Earl and I am also a first year student. Let me introduce you to the guys."

Earl was about 6'3", light in completion with a slim body frame. As the conversation continued throughout the afternoon, I got to know more about Earl. He loved action movies just like I did. From there on we met in the laboratory any time we had practical software programing lesson. After a while, I began to notice something unusual about him. It seemed that he was always in the laboratory before anyone else. "What could he be up to?" I asked myself. "What must he be doing alone in the lab?" I decided to ask him.

"Hello! Earl, how come you are always in the laboratory and whenever everyone else leaves, you don't leave? What is it you are doing on your laptop with your headphones on?"

"Hello, police man! I did not know I am being followed." He replied.

"It is just a question. You don't have to reply"

"I am downloading movies."

"Downloading movies, what sort of movies are you downloading?" I asked as I settled down to look at his laptop screen.

"Action and porn movies, He smiled. "I hope you know what porn movies are, Ty."

"Oh yes! I know what porn movies are." Of course I did. It had been my occupation every night for over many years.

He looked at me and said, "You don't sound surprised?"

"Sound surprised? About what?" I answered.

"That I am downloading porn."

"Why should I? Is it not a man thing? Every man I know watches porn". I could not believe what I was hearing. Did he just say downloading movies? How could that be possible?

"Are you okay, Ty?"

"Oh sorry, Earl,"

"It seems you are in a deep thought," he said.

"Sorry I was just thinking about something." My mind had drifted into thinking about the possibility of having easy access to loads of porn movies.

"I hope everything is okay," he replied.

"Oh! Everything is fine, Earl. Could you please show me how to download movies from the internet?"

"You mean download porn movies?" he said with a grin on his face. "Don't tell me you don't like porn. Every guy I know likes porn".

"Yes. I do watch porn but not that much." I lied! "I have got some DVDs but not that many."

"Nice Ty! Could you bring one for me tomorrow, if that is okay?"

"Sure, no problem. I could do that. But, will you show me how to download movies from the internet?" I asked.

"Ty, I will show if you only stop telling me you only want to download movies. I know you really would like me to show you how to download porn from the internet as well," he said smiling knowingly.

"Of course," I replied trying to hide my desperation.

"Let's meet same time tomorrow. I am very sure you will be here before me". He smiled as he assured me, "I will be here, Ty".

On my way home, I could not but think about what Earl had just said. *How is that possible? How can he be downloading porn from the internet free, without paying a dime when I was buying DVDs every time? This is too good to be true. I have to learn how to download from the internet, so that I can watch as much porn as I want without paying ever again.* As soon as I got back home, I immediately put the DVD in my bag ready for tomorrow as promised. The last thing I wanted to do was to forget.

As usual, night time was my masturbating time. While lying in bed I could not but think about how soon I too would be able to download porn on the internet. This, to me, was the best thing that could have ever happen to me.

The next day, I woke up with excitement. I could not just wait to see Earl. I dressed up quickly, double checked my bag just to ensure the DVD was there and off I was. My entire body was excited. I kept telling myself, "Today, I too will be able to download porn from the internet."

I headed straight for the university computer laboratory even though I had a lecture to attend. "It doesn't matter," I told myself. Entering the laboratory, Earl was nowhere to be found. *He promised he would be here! What is going on? Doesn't he know how important this is for me?* I had to call him on his mobile phone. *Why isn't he picking up his phone?* I was getting agitated. I decided to leave a message for him telling him I was waiting for him in the laboratory.

About an hour later, Earl finally showed up. "Ty, I am really sorry. I went to bed very late last night that was why I couldn't meet you as agreed?" I could barely keep my calm but just managed to say, "No problem. Can we get to the business of the day?"

"'Wow, Ty! You cannot even wait till lunch time!"

"Wait? No way," I replied.

"But I thought you said you don't like porn that much, so why the rush?"

"Am I in rushing?"

"Yes Ty! But that is okay. Let's crack on." He placed his laptop on the table and logged on.

"Actually, you were meant to bring a DVD for me as part of our agreement. I hope you did not forget?"

"No! I did not." I brought out the DVD and handed it to him.

"This is nice, Ty. I don't think I have seen this before. I will have to add it to the collection I have got."

"Collection? How many DVDs have you got? I asked trying to hide my excitement.

"Not many but more than you could think," he replied casually.

"Come on please tell me how big a collection you have?"

"Around 200 gigabyte"

"200 gigabyte of porn" The revelation shocked me to the bone

"Yes, is that too much?"

"No," I replied trying my best to sound calm. Excitement was getting the better of me.

"But, the way you reacted sounded as if it's too much."

"No, I was just shocked you have that much."

"Can you upload some for me?"

"Why not? But, let me finish your setup for you first."

"200 gigabyte" wow"

"Come on, Ty! You sound as if that is a lot. I have got friends with more."

"In our year" He has got friends with more?!

"Yes!"

"You need to introduce me to them."

"Ty, chill out. Why are you so excited all of a sudden?"

"I just can't believe there are people with more than 200 gigabyte of porn in our year!"

"Ty, if we go on this way, I would not be able to finish your download set-up."

"Sorry!"

"Ty, I want you to write down some of these websites because you will need them when I am not around to help."

After completing the set-up, I asked him to wait behind for me to go through it. To ensure there were no set-up errors, I asked Earl to take me through it again. "Ty, do you think I don't know what I am doing?" he asked.

"Come on, Earl! I just want to make sure it's properly working" I replied.

My excitement of downloading porn from the internet was so much. I decided I was going to spend the entire day in the laboratory and catch up with the lectures I had missed later. Earl hadn't gotten to the exit door of the laboratory before I began downloading porn from the internet; it seemed I had just won a jackpot!

Who needs porn magazine with these internet sites? This was a whole new world, a place where I could access thousands and thousands of images at a click without paying for them. *Why didn't I know about this while in school or college?*

By mid-session of my first year at university, I was spending four to five hours minimum a day downloading images and porn movies from the internet. I had started looking for things I would not have watched while I was younger, things so gross that after I had finished watching and masturbating to the porn movie I would ask myself, "Who could have watched this type of movie? A normal person just would not have watched this kind of movie."

My daily routine now involved coming into the laboratory early every morning just before lectures to connect my laptop to the internet to download porn. In order to spend more time downloading, I also began skipping lectures without caring about the consequence. When that wasn't enough, I started leaving my laptop behind to download more porn. The thought of someone stealing my laptop didn't even cross my mind. My only goal each day was simply to download porn, masturbate and visit prostitutes.

Attending lectures was becoming tiresome as it seemed my only interest was in downloading more porn. Each time I watched a new porn movie, I felt it wasn't good enough and there should be something better than that one. I was looking for something new every single day. The only thing I began to care more and more about was how I could download even more porn movies. I just never had enough.

While lectures were going on, I would find myself imagining what the movie I was downloading would be like. Throughout the lectures, I was in a world of my own and everything around me was irrelevant. Anything other than downloading porn became totally uninteresting to me.

As time went by, word began to get round that I might be sleeping in the lab. Some of my classmates began to tease me about downloading porn for them. Some even asked if I could transfer it on to their memory stick or even burn it on to CD or DVD. Soon, I was carrying about 400 gigabyte of porn. This made me one of the biggest collectors of porn in my class.

5

THE MAN WITHOUT A BRAIN

Progress in life is a function of the brain.
When the brain is infected with porn,
life becomes stagnated.

Repeat?! How on earth could that be possible? Those marks couldn't have been correct! I will have to see my professor as soon as possible. There is no way I could fail those exams. Those exams were too simple for me to fail.

"Are you alright, Ty," asked my friend.

"Alright? I am fine. I am fine," I replied.

"It seems you are having a conversation with yourself. How was your result?"

"Not very good."

"What do you mean by that?"

"It says I failed some of my modules."

"How could that be? You are very smart guy, Ty!"

"That was what I was saying to myself just before you came in!"

While we stood in the corridor lamenting, my lecturer walked in. "Good morning Ty!" he said as he walked past us. "What are you doing here so early?"

"Sir, my exam result," I muttered.

"What is wrong with your exam result?"

"It says 'repeat', sir!"

"Ty!"

"Yes, sir!"

"But, those were your true marks. I am really sorry to hear that but you will just have to repeat the class next year."

"Sir, I did very well in those exams. There is no way I could have failed them, sir! Is there any way I could check if all my course work was added up correctly, sir?" I was enveloped in total disbelief.

"Are you implying your tutors don't know how to add up numbers?" clearly, my lecturer wasn't happy with the way I was challenging my results

"No sir! That wasn't what I meant."

"But, that is what your tone sounds like, Ty!" He peered at me disapprovingly and said, "Your scores have all been totalled up correctly; every exam paper had to be checked by another marker before marks were awarded. So, my advice for you will be to ensure you are ready for next term. Make sure you don't miss any lecture; and, if you think you are struggling with any of your modules, then, let me know so we can do something about it. Unfortunately, there is nothing I can do to help. You will just have to repeat the class, Ty."

It seemed someone had just ripped my heart apart with those words! It felt like an extra weight had been added to my legs. I had to find myself a seat or else I would've collapsed. *What had just happened? How could I have failed those exams? I knew I missed some lectures but that couldn't have been the reason! Could it have been the porn I had been watching? But, I did stop watching porn just before my exams. That couldn't have had any impact on my result. I think it's about time I stop watching porn and focus on my studies. If I continue what I did this year, I am sure the next year will be the same. I have got to stop now before is too late.*

So, before my exams I made a decision. I was going to delete all porn movies I had on my laptop, throw away all of my DVDs and focus on my upcoming exam. Straightaway, as soon as I had deleted those movies I started downloading more. I knew something was wrong. But, the more I tried to stop, the more it seemed I was getting deeper. I even began watching some gruesome materials that even I myself found very disgusting after watching them.

I had always seen myself as smart and all I needed was just a quick revision and everything would be okay. But, my worst fear had just been confirmed. *Repeat! How could someone like me repeat a class?*

On my journey back home, I decided I wasn't going to tell my brother or anyone else that I had just failed my exams. And, most importantly I decided I was going to get rid of all the porn materials. I was going to have a new beginning, a new resolution for the year. But, as soon as I got back home, the struggle of getting rid of them was just too much. I tried and pushed myself really hard to delete all the porn materials I had on my laptop. Not long after deleting them, I started downloading more porn movies but this time, I was spending twice the hours I would usually spend.

I never for once saw myself as someone with a porn problem, even though the time I spent watching porn had spiralled out of control. I could easily lock myself up in my room watching porn and masturbating all day without coming out of my house, which wasn't a problem as far as I was concerned. However I began to sense there was something wrong with my thoughts and thinking pattern. It appeared the only thing I could think about was porn and masturbating. Even when lectures were going on, all my thoughts were about porn movies. *When am I going to watch it? Have I seen it before? Will I like it? Will I be able to masturbate to it?* That was all I could think about.

One day on my way home, I had planned to do some food shopping but on getting to the supermarket, I had totally forgotten what I was there for. There I was standing right in the middle of the supermarket and I could not remember what I planned to buy! It was like my memory had switched off. I couldn't just remember what I had planned to do. *What is wrong with me? What is it I planned I was going to do?* I left the supermarket without buying anything. It was when I arrived home that I remembered that there was no food at home; but I knew this before leaving the house. *What is going on with me?* That day was just the beginning of my nightmare.

Soon I was struggling to understand things or how things work. Each time I was about to think of anything unrelated to porn and masturbating, my entire brain would shut down. I could not process anything aside from porn and masturbating. It was as if there was a mental cap blocking my frontal brain. *What could be happening to me?* Each time I planned to carry out an activity, I would have to masturbate in order to get the energy I needed to do what I originally planned. Reading or studying then became my biggest challenge. In order to read, I would have to watch porn and masturbate. Without doing that, it seemed the strength and focus I needed to engage my brain was just not there. It seemed I was just carrying an empty shell of a brain on my neck.

6

OVERPOWERING DESIRE

Embedded within every desire is seed which will either influence you in positive or negative ways.

I had always been the one to determine when I watched porn, masturbated or slept with prostitutes. It got to the point where, getting rid of these thoughts had become a challenge. The persistent, strong thoughts of masturbating wouldn't just go away. Before it seemed I could think about masturbating whenever I wanted. Now it was as if the masturbating thoughts were controlling my everyday life.

I spent more time watching porn than I spent on my studies. Not only that, I began to view women as ordinary sex objects. Whenever I saw a lady I particularly liked in a porn movie, I began to look for the same features in every lady I met. I would go around storing their images in my mind and later I would masturbate using the images, a process I had discovered and perfected over time. Most importantly, I had learnt that there is no limit to the number of images I could store in my mind. I could keep storing and storing and never exhaust the space in my mind. My daily goal was to search for women with the same features as the ladies in the porn movie and store them to be used later.

Something drastic began to change each time I masturbated before going to bed. I was struggling to get an erection. The lady I was masturbating with in my mind wasn't stimulating me enough. What normally took me about 15 minutes to erect was beginning to take hours. *What is wrong? Why am I not having an erection?* Before I knew what was happening, the alarm clock would go off and it would be 1 am and I still couldn't bring myself to erect. When I finally got an erection, it would then take some more hours to ejaculate. This wasn't happening before. Eventually, my everyday became filled with looking for women that will make me ejaculate quicker while masturbating.

In addition, I was having problems with the number of hours I spent looking for porn movies. What would have taken 30 minutes was now taking three to four hours. At first, it was just about watching porn and imagining myself masturbating with the ladies in the videos. But, eventually just any lady in a porn movie wasn't enough. I didn't mind wandering from one porn store to the next searching for DVDs with ladies who had the specific features I desired. I would not stop until I had found one. I just had to find it! I kept telling myself that particular DVD will make me to erect quicker. But, on getting home I would realise that wasn't the case because I just could not get myself to erect as quickly as I would have liked to. This intensified my drive to search the streets, clubs and bars for ladies that matched the ones in the porn movie. My number one mission had become to search for ladies I could use for masturbating every night. The images I already had in my mind couldn't stimulate me any longer. It was important that I got something that could stimulate me in order to erect and ejaculate quicker. Otherwise, there is no chance of me sleeping that night.

As time went by, things became even worse. If I came across any lady that matched the image in my mind, straightaway I would cancel all my appointments no matter how important they were. I could be anywhere – train, bus, club, pub. If my phone rang, no matter who was calling and how important the call might be, I would ignore it. My focus would be on the lady, shutting out the rest of the world. Nothing else mattered in the world but the lady in front of me. Once it was night time, I would replay all the female images I had stored in my mind during the day to see which one I could conjure up to help me erect and ejaculate quicker. It was as if I was going through a photo album or pictures saved on a memory stick.

I would lie in bed for at least four hours going through pictures of various ladies to see which one I could masturbate to and before I knew it, the sun would begin to rise. I would have spent the night going through my mental database of pictures and would end up not finding a satisfactory image that will cause me to erect. By the time I get myself to erect and ejaculate, I would be so exhausted that I would desperately need to sleep. This means I would have to cancel all my activities including lectures even before the day begins. Waking up at midday is the most gruesome task ever, because even though I must have had seven to eight hours sleep, it would seem like I had been on a weightlifting program and my entire body would be aching.

Watching porn used to be fun but it eventually became a plight to find a certain type of woman to masturbate to. I began to watch certain kinds of porn movies which were now becoming filthier! Dangerous activities were carried out on women which were so disgusting that I just had to destroy the DVD after watching it. *How can a normal human engage in such filth and put their body through a process that could even kill them?* But, the next day I would be back in the store looking for something even worse than what I had seen the day before. Nothing would stop me from buying the same DVD or a different one.

Looking for prostitutes had become like a trip to the supermarket, moving through each shelf looking for a product or brand better than the other. I would knock on the doors of different prostitutes to see which one of them matched the kind of picture I had in my brain. Some didn't even know that was what I was doing as I asked questions such as, "How much does a session cost?" While I talked to each prostitute, I'd be going through all the pictures in my mind trying to see if they match any of those images. If I didn't feel they were a match, I would move to the next one because sleeping with a prostitute is based on time. If a prostitute finds out that you can't have an erection or ejaculate within the time you have paid for, she would tell you to leave because there are other customers waiting for her service. It is not her fault you can't have an erection. Every time I slept with a prostitute, I aimed to get it right. Otherwise, I would pay without enjoying the sex I paid for.

7

LIVING ON THE STREET

Soho town, located within central London is made up streets lined with offices, restaurants, pubs, night clubs, sex shops, prostitutes' homes and strip bars. The early hours of the day in Soho town can be quite deceiving. You'd see well-dressed people from all walks of life heading towards their respective offices. If you're a tourist visiting during the day, you might be deceived into thinking that it's a boring place to visit; but, come evening time, it seems the whole country has been invited to a carnival. Street lights alive everywhere, blaring music coming from various pubs and tourists staring at the massive advertising billboards.

Soho town had become like a second home to me where I spent most of my time after lectures. I have covered every street visiting possibly every prostitute's home, strip clubs and sex shops of various kinds. Seeing me in Soho, no tourist would know that I lived in UK. They would look at me and think I was a tourist too because of the bag around my neck.

Life was really good. I felt I was having the best time of my life savouring all Soho could possibly offer but things weren't really as they seemed. An onlooker would take a look at me and think I was here just to enjoy the beautiful Victorian buildings that lined the streets. They would never guess I was always here every day doing the same thing over and over again.

My love of Soho town started when I discovered I could easily access the prostitutes' services. When I discovered Soho it was as if I had hit a jackpot. Prostitutes were everywhere. Every house was either used for prostitution or for selling sex items. I began to spend my entire day roaming about the town going from one end to another. If you know the size of this place, you would attest that it's not a small town with a couple of roads. Driven by my insatiable desire for porn, I rummaged through the streets not knowing what I was looking for. There were times I would find myself on a dead end street or in an alley way and wonder how I ended up there.

Six hours on the streets of Soho and I would still be moving from one sex shop to another, swinging from one strip bar to another still not knowing exactly what I was looking for. *What was driving me? Am I trying to satisfy an insatiable sexual urge?* I didn't know the answer to this question myself.

Soon, I became well-known within the community of prostitutes. I was truly a well-known regular and not only that, I had favourite prostitutes. There were some I liked visiting every day; there were some I'd only visit when my favourites were busy with other customers. All I needed was to pick up my phone. Flicking through my contact list, you would think I had many female friends; but, most of the numbers were for my prostitutes. All I needed to do whenever I wanted to visit was simply to call and say, "Hey! I am coming over tonight. Are you going to be available?" If I turned up and realised they were busy, I would wait until their customer leaves.

Several rounds of sex with girlfriends at university weren't enough. There was this strong uncontrollable desire for more sex even though I really did not want to. Notwithstanding, I would head for Soho for another round of sex. My first port of call would normally be to visit the sex shop and look through all the magazines on display. Next, I'd move on to the sex movie cinema to see a porn movie just to increase my sexual urge before dropping in for another sex session with a prostitute.

On my way home from lectures, I'd typically tell myself how tired I was and that all I needed was to get indoors to watch porn, masturbate and sleep. Just as I am about to make a decision to go home, the usual urge that compels me to go to Soho town would spring up. *Could I afford to spend any money today?* Even if the answer was no, I'd tell myself that I will just go anyway and that I will not buy any porn DVD or porn magazine or sleep with any prostitutes. But, as soon as I stepped into Soho, I would forget everything I had said and end up sleeping with a prostitute.

When I started visiting Soho, I would usually spend an hour or two walking around the town. There were times I would be there for four or five hours doing nothing but walking around. Sometimes I would still be there at 11 pm.

So many times I said to myself that I really need to go home but it seemed I was just totally overpowered by the desire to have sex even though I really didn't want to. I couldn't just stop myself. *I haven't got much in my account. I need to do food shopping but I feel I need to have sex before I leave. This is going to cost me dearly. What do I do now? Maybe I should get a porn DVD instead rather than having sex tonight.* I knew I couldn't afford the movie. I knew there wasn't any food at home. I knew I didn't have much left in my account to live on till my next student loan was paid. but then, I would go into the shop and say, "Sir, could I please pay for these two movies?"

It would be about 11.30 pm and I still wouldn't have eaten anything all afternoon. *I am really starving but can't afford a burger. I think am just going to manage myself until I get home.* Then I get home and there is nothing good in the house to eat. My stupidity would stare me in the face. I am left with nothing for the rest of the month. My brother should not know about this. I am really disgusted with myself. *Am I okay? Something must be wrong with me otherwise why have I bought these DVDs? There is nothing special about this movie anyway.* I even promised myself I wasn't going to spend a penny from my account but now I am left with nothing, just what will get me through university for the rest of the month.

8

SOMEBODY CALL THE AMBULANCE

*You only have one life; be careful not to waste it.
You might not have a second chance.*

I was back in Soho again. What am I doing here? This should be the last place I would ever come to after what has just happen to me in the last couple of days. I was just recovering from what the doctor called poisoning. I really didn't want to be here but there was this strong desire that kept propelling me to come back to this place. I kept telling myself I didn't want to be there. What am I doing here? I should be resting. No problem then. Now that I am here, what I will do is to just stay away from prostitutes.

This time around I was determined that no matter what it would cost me, I wasn't going to sleep with any prostitute. Instead, I would go home to sleep. But, a fierce battle was raging within me and so I just could not resist the desire to knock on the prostitute's door. She opened the door and said, "Hello Ty. How are you doing? I haven't seen you for a couple of days now. Would you like to come for the usual?" I replied, "I just want to check if you are in but will come back later." That day, I succeeded in not sleeping with a prostitute but still ended up buying a porn movie.

By the time I got back home, I was so tired and weak from walking around all day. I settled down to watch the porn movie like I always would but this time it just seemed I was tired of everything; tired of life and what my life had turned into. *There must be other ways to come out of this because right now, I don't know if I am a sex addict or a porn junkie. Something must happen or else my life is in ruins.*

The following day, I reflected on my predicament days before. I still could not understand how the drug could have turned into poison. What actually happened? I remembered watching a porn movie that afternoon. While watching the movie, I kept thinking to myself that I wished I could spend longer hours having sex like those guys in the movie. I played with this thought for a long time before I decided I would go to Soho to try what I had seen in the porn movie.

I remember I located my regular shop where I normally bought porn movies and porn magazines. Stepping into the store that very afternoon the only thing on my mind was how I could try out what I had seen in the porn movie. I remember approaching the sales assistant and asking him if they had sex drugs that could make you 'go for longer rounds', and he pointed to the shelves. I walked towards the display shelves. There were various bottles arranged according to colour. I picked one of the bottles to read what was written on it and what it does. I still cannot remember the instructions. I was only thinking about getting something and using it. There was nothing on the bottle to say you will have sex for longer if you take it.

I picked one in a small bottle with a red label on top and took it to the counter to make payment. After stepping out of the shop, I turned the bottle around to read the instructions on it. It clearly stated the drug must be taken with food but by then, I was so zoned into what I really wanted to do that I decided to ignore the instruction. I headed straight to my favourite prostitute. Like I would always do, I had already called the prostitute to tell her I was coming. I told her that I was going to spend quite a few hours with her and that she should ensure that she is free when I get there.

After pouring the entire bottle down my throat, I began to feel dizzy immediately. I thought nothing of it. As I walked through the prostitute's open door, she asked if I was okay and I nodded indicating that I was. I said that there was nothing wrong and that I was only feeling a little bit dizzy. She suggested that I rest for a while but I ignored her and told her to let us get on with the main action of the day. While we had sex, I realised the dizziness was getting worse. Immediately, she realised I was struggling for breath she asked me to leave.

I remember I sat down on her chair as she was telling me to leave quickly. Soon, I was gasping for breath. It seemed I would collapse. I managed to find my way down the stairs and make my way towards the street. On approaching a street adjacent to a place called Leicester Square, I found myself holding the street light pole. I couldn't move but tried leaning on it for support. Then I remembered slipping down the pole and before I knew what was going on, I was flat on the floor clinging to life.

The only thing I could see was a man wearing a kind of black jacket touching me and trying to get my attention. He was asking if I was okay but by then I couldn't reply as my eyes were shutting. I heard someone shout, "Somebody call the ambulance. A man has just collapsed in the street". I could remember one of the emergency officers trying to get some answers out of me but before I could reply I just passed out.

The next time I opened my eyes to say something, I realised there was an oxygen mask over my face. As I tried to remove it, one of the nurses walked towards me to help me take it off. When I asked her what I was doing there, she said the emergency unit brought me in and said they found me collapsed in the street. *Collapsed! How could that happen?* The nurse knew I was trying to stand from the bed and told me to stay put on my back. Turning to my right, I saw drips connected to my veins. *How could this happen?* I couldn't answer but while that thought was going through my mind, I dozed off.

Next morning, I woke up still trying to figure out answers to the questions on my mind. *What could have happened?* While engrossed in my thoughts, about seven doctors came to stand beside my bed. One of the doctors, who I believe was the leader of the pack, asked me why I wanted to commit suicide.

"Suicide? I do not want to commit suicide," I replied. What he said next sounded as if a bullet was shot into me.

"Your blood test shows you took poison."

"Poison? Why would I want to take poison," I asked.

"But that was what was found in your system. Would you like us to contact any of your family members and let them know you are here?"

"No. I will be okay."

I do not know what drew my attention to my palm but when I looked at it, it had turned green. I was really scared. I wanted to jump up when the doctor held me down and said I should not worry that it will clear off. I was left in shock. *Where did the poison come from?* Then it dawned on me that the sex drug I took had turned into poison. *But how could that have happened?* I really could not explain it, but I knew I could not tell anyone about what had just happened. Not even my girlfriend or family must know about it.

I was discharged from the hospital at about 12 pm. Making my way home, I couldn't get the thoughts off my mind. *How would a sex drug turn into poison?* On getting home, I looked round to see if my younger brother was in but he wasn't. I stepped into the toilet to urinate and then I realised I was passing out green fluid. *Where is green coming from?* I was so scared to see what was coming out of my penis. I screamed. Then I remembered what the doctor said, "It would take a couple of weeks to clean out the poison from your system".

9

IS THIS STD?!!!

*A brain full of porn will only
produce a life full of porn activities*

"We have looked through your blood and urine samples, Mr Ty. I am afraid the test did not show what exactly is wrong with you. What I can do, is prescribe you with some antibiotics and if there is no change after a week, then I would have to send you to a specialist to carry out a further test".

"What about the constant pain?" I asked.

"That is why I am prescribing some antibiotics to relieve the pain."

"But, what about the swelling sir?"

"Unfortunately, I would not be able to prescribe anything for the swelling at the moment, Mr Ty."

"Are you implying that I would have to wait for a week?"

"Like I said, Mr Ty, there is nothing I can do at the moment. What I will say Mr Ty, is wait, and if the swelling remains then I will send you to a specialist".

What exactly is causing this swelling? Could I have contracted this from sleeping with prostitutes? Could it be a sexually transmitted disease? Could it be because I masturbate every day? If this swelling does not reduce after a week, then I am in real trouble. What would happen to me if by next week this swelling does not reduce and further test says I have got STD? My heart was pounding so fast I could literally hear the beating sound.

Back home from the hospital, the only thing I could do to get my mind off the pain was to masturbate again! Looking at my manhood and seeing how swollen it was, I decided it would be dangerous for me to masturbate. I didn't want to do it to myself but I couldn't prevent myself from masturbating. As soon as I finished, the swollen area burst open and blood was everywhere. *My God, my God! Who will help me out of this addiction?* I began to cry. *Is there anybody out there that can please help me? This pain is too unbearable. I really don't feel like masturbating but I cannot stop myself. Will I die with this?* That day I cried myself to bed.

"How are you doing today?" the doctor asked when I returned to hospital after a week.

"Not very good, sir"

"Has the swelling reduced?"

"No. Still swollen and the pain hasn't stopped either"

"I think it will be better to send you to a specialist to check exactly what is wrong with you."

"In your years of practise, have you seen such a thing before?" I asked the doctor.

"Not really," the doctor replied. "I wish I could give you

the answer but honestly it is not something I have ever dealt with before."

The day for my appointment with the specialist arrived. I hoped I would be able to get answers and whatever the result I hope it won't show that it was masturbating that caused it.

"Good morning. My name is Ty. I have got an appointment today." The receptionist motioned me to sit and went off to get the doctor. This was it. I thought whatever happened I knew I was leaving with a result.

"Good morning, Mr Ty! Is everything okay?" The doctor's face gave nothing away to alleviate my anxiety.

"Everything is fine." I replied as I came out of my deep thoughts.

"It appears you are in deep thought."

"Not really. I am just concerned about the swelling around my penis."

"You shouldn't worry, Mr Ty. I have gone through your report and hopefully we will be able to get to the bottom of the situation. Could you please remove your trousers and pants for me, Mr Ty, and let me carry out some checks. I have never seen this type of swelling before. When did you notice it?"

"About two weeks ago while having my bath," I replied.

"Have you ever had this kind of problem before?"

"Not really," I replied.

"Okay! Let me extract some blood and urine samples which should return in 40 to 60 minutes."

In the next 60 minutes my fate would be determined, but I decided that after that day everything called masturbating must stop.

"Hello, Mr Ty! I have got your results. Are you pleased to know what the report says?"

"Yes and maybe."

"Anyway your result is negative. Your blood is clean and there is nothing showing in your urine."

"That sounds good," I replied.

"What I would say is maybe you are reacting to something?"

"React? I don't normally react to things", I replied.

"I would suggest that you continue using the antibiotics and hopefully the swelling would reduce".

Thank God! I didn't have STD but who will ever get married to someone with porn and masturbating habits? What would happen if I got married and my wife caught me masturbating and she realised I am unable to get an erection without watching porn. What would she say? I couldn't stop thinking about how my life would have turned out well if I wasn't introduced to porn.

10

I AM BROKE

How come my bank balance is £100? The last time I checked it was £600. I haven't done the house shopping I promised to do. I haven't shopped for clothes neither even though all my clothes need changing; but, that is not the point now. Someone must have gained access into my account and withdrawn the balance of my student loan. Maybe my brother has taken some money out but he hasn't got access to my back details. What could have happened? I haven't spent any money lately.

Confused, I decided to check when the money had been withdrawn, and possibly that would give me a clue as to who had taken the money. If I didn't get this money back as soon as possible I would be broke till the end the year. *How am I going to survive?*

What is this I am seeing? 'Web pay, web pay….' Who is web pay? I haven't bought anything from the internet lately who can web pay be? Believing someone must have gained access to my personal details without my consent and taken the money, I called my bank straight away. I was shouting at the guy on the line.

"Someone has taken my money. How did the bank allow that to happen?"

"Mr Kolade, could you please let me have your details and ask you some security questions before I can be of help? Mr Kolade, do you know anything about web pay?"

I replied emphatically with, "No. Why would I know web pay? Could you see they have taken money out of my account every day? My statement is even saying every minute. How could the bank allow that to happen to my account?"

The next line that came from the guy at the other end of the phone just felt like someone had poured a bucket of water on my head. He asked, "Do you know about a sex website?"

"What sex website are you talking about?"

"It seems you have been using your account to purchase something from a sex website."

"I am afraid I don't know what that could be." I didn't know when I dropped the phone and held my head in my two hands.

What have I just done? Did I just spend over £500 downloading porn movies online? How did that happen? Right there and then, I knew I had a problem. I was not working and had blown all I had on watching porn. I didn't know how I was going to get through the year. *What is wrong with me? I think I need help.*

11

WHY THE GUILT?

Ask a prisoner the definition of freedom.
He or she will tell you it's not found in the dictionary

What exactly could be happening to me? Instead of feeling refreshed, I was feeling so tired. It appeared I had just got back from a jogging exercise. Even after eight hours sleep, I was still very tired. *Why am I so fretful about everything, constantly thinking something bad would happen to me?* At that point I didn't expect anything good from life.

My heartbeat was racing so fast only God knew what exactly could be wrong with me. Won't it be nice if I could just lie down here and not worry about anything and life just remains perfect? I wish I never met the Genesis group! I regretted the day I met up with G to watch porn. I wish everything could have been good with my parents and I could ask them about anything and everything. I wish they knew all I needed then was just their love and nothing else, how things would have turn out for the best.

There was a knock on the door. I wasn't expecting anyone. Immediately, my heart began to beat so fast it seemed I would collapse as I approached the door. I peeped through the door hole and it was Kelvin. "It is you Kelvin", I said.

"What is wrong with you Ty? Why do you look so fearful? You're not the type that gets scared. And, why are you breathing so heavily?" Kevin asked.

"Nothing, friend, I wasn't just expecting anybody today," I replied.

"But the way you are breathing is not the best, Ty. You don't look well. I hope everything is okay?"

"I am fine. I just need some rest."

"Ty, I think you should come to church with me next Sunday. It appears each time I come to your house all you do is watch football all day.

"I don't think that it is your problem what I do with my time, and I would appreciate it if you would not talk about me coming to your church each time you come to my house. Did I tell you I needed help?"

"Don't take it personally, Ty. I was only suggesting."

"I will appreciate it if you keep your church out of our discussion."

Kelvin knew I liked watching porn and he was always teasing me about getting myself a wife instead of watching porn.

"I hope you are not masturbating, Ty, because everyone that watches porn always masturbates."

I said, "Because I watch porn doesn't mean I masturbate" but deep inside I knew I was struggling with it. Just before he arrived I had already masturbated but there was no way I would have told him I was struggling with masturbation. He would probably laugh and make fun of me.

Later Kelvin decided it was time to leave and as he was leaving he turned around and said, "Ty, next Sunday I will be here to pick you up for church and you must be ready". I closed the door behind him. *I don't know who told him I needed help! Maybe he is right. I will follow him to church next Sunday. Maybe the church could help.*

I knew I had tried everything I could to stop watching porn but no self-help had worked. Each time I tried to stop, I found myself coming back with a stronger desire for more hard core porn than before. I could not understand how I started out watching simple porn but 10 years down the line, I found myself watching something a normal person in their right mind shouldn't be watching. I knew I had to be free from this habit before I did something very terrible which I would later regret in life.

I thought maybe the church could actually help me. I just wanted to be free. I really needed peace of mind. I wanted to be free from anxiety and fear, fear that something really bad was going to happen to me.

Just as Kelvin had promised, his phone call woke me up on Sunday.

"What are you doing calling me so early on Sunday morning? Isn't it the weekend for crying out load? 8 am?" I said.

"Ty, I promised I was going to pick you up for church today. Remember"

"But not this early!, could we not go later and why so early?" I replied.

"Ty, I am coming to pick you up and you have got to be ready before I get there."

As inconvenient as it was, I decided I would go to see what Kelvin's church was like. Maybe the preacher would be able to solve my problem. After all, there was no cost to it.

As we approached the church, I noticed quite a number of cars parked along the road.

"Why are there so many cars outside at a very early hour of Sunday morning? Are you sure you are not taking me to a club," I said.

"Ty, why do you think I will bring you to a club?" Kelvin replied.

At the church entrance we were welcomed by ladies opening the door and ushering us in with a smile. *This must be a club! Where on earth do you find beautiful ladies opening the door for you to come inside? This cannot be church.* I had only ever seen this sort of thing in clubs, bars and concerts.

Stepping inside, I met the greatest shock of my life. Hundreds of people were sitting down waiting for the church service to begin. *Are these people okay?* I turned to Kelvin, "What kind of church is this?" I asked. By now, my interest was focused only on the ladies. Throughout the church service and even when the preacher was teaching, my eyes fed on the beautiful ladies around me. I could not remember exactly what was taught or said. I just kept saying to myself that this church had a lot of beautiful ladies. I was already trying to identify which ladies had the features I could store in mind and use to have imaginary sex when I got back home. Before the service was over, I was already imagining myself with the ladies, assessing which one of them will give me a quick erection. By the time the service was over, I was ready to go and masturbate to my selection.

Two months after my first visit to the church, I decided to visit again. I really don't know why I went back there but I did. This time around it wasn't as packed as the first time I came. In my mind, I was asking where all the beautiful ladies and women I saw the first time I came were. I decided I would sit through the service not knowing why I made the choice. During the church service, I began to have a strong desire to watch porn. The desire was so strong that I thought I just had to leave or else I would have to run into the toilets and masturbate. But, while I battled with my thoughts, I noticed everyone was standing on their feet as the preacher was approaching the stand. So, I decided to stand as well even though I didn't know what was happening. *Why are they standing?* Just as I was about to sit down, the preacher then asked us to sing, Sing? *I don't like singing.* I told myself that I was definitely not coming back to this church ever again.

Singing finished, the preacher began to preach. I could not remember exactly what he said because I was just thinking about the porn movie I planned to watch when I got back home. Just as he was rounding up his teaching, he said something that caught my attention.

"Is there anyone here tonight that is not sure of what tomorrow holds? You seem tired and lost. Everywhere around you seems dark and doom. You know if you leave here tonight it might be too late. Please step outside and give your life to Jesus."

Hold on, preacher! How do you know what I am going through? I hadn't spoken to him about my problem so there was no way he could have known anything about me. That aside, *what can this Jesus he is talking about do for me anyway?* I had heard about this Jesus while I was growing up. I even used to read about him in Bible stories at Sunday school and there I was being told Jesus in the bible stories can help me overcome porn and masturbation. *What does this Jesus know about porn anyway?* I really did not think he would be interested in someone that sleeps with prostitutes. Moreover I had been told Jesus can be angry with you if you do something wrong. And all my life I had always been doing wrong. *So why would I want Jesus to punish me again? No way! Jesus can hold Himself because the last thing I need from Him is for Him to be angry with me.* My parents were always angry with me while I was young. The last thing I needed was for this Jesus to also be angry with me.

It seemed this preacher was talking directly to me even though I hadn't said anything to him. So why in the world would he be saying exactly what I am going through? Not only that, he was even asking me to come out. I wondered what would happen if I stepped out. *Will these people laugh at me? They would probably be thinking, "Look at this guy with earrings and plaits going forward."* I said to myself, "Maybe I will just sit this one out. Just as I was completing the statement I heard something say, "Today is your last chance." *What? Who in the world is telling me today is my last chance? Why would today be my last chance anyways? Who are you to tell me today is my last chance.*

Who was it that might have spoken to me? I looked at the person sitting next to me. I noticed his eyes were tightly shut. *What!* I turned to the next person. Her eyes were shut as well. *No way, who is it that could have just told me today is my last chance? Maybe I am hearing myself.* Again, I heard the same words: "Today is your last chance." This time around I thought I must be going insane. I became so frightened that I decided to stand up; maybe the person playing the prank would stop.

As soon as I stood up, I felt someone touch my shoulder. *Not again!* I was so scared I refused to open my eyes. Again, I felt someone touch me on the shoulder. This time I opened my eyes slightly to see who it might be and there was a man gently signalling to me to come out. I pointed my finger at myself to confirm whether he was really talking to me. He nodded and mouthed a yes. I stepped out of my seat and followed the gentleman as he led me out towards the preacher. At that moment, I was thinking that this whole church would soon burst into laughter but instead they were clapping for me. I was puzzled. *Why are they clapping? Do they know me from anywhere? Why are you all clapping for me? There must be something wrong with these people.*

As I stood in front of the preacher, he looked at me and said, "You are welcome." I nodded my head. "Welcome to where?" I said to myself. Then he said I should repeat the *following* prayers after him. "Repeat what prayers?" I thought to myself. I was so conscious of the environment. I found it hard to concentrate on whatever prayers the preacher asked me to pray. I was so conscious of the whole church looking at me strangely. I just mumbled whatever prayer I was asked to pray. The preacher looked at me and smiled. Then he said, "Welcome to the family of Jesus." I said within myself, "What family?"

The preacher then asked me to turn around and follow the man that led me to the front. I followed the man, who by then was smiling but I couldn't help wondering why this man was smiling. As soon as I sat down with the gentleman, he handed me a form to fill in and said someone would contact me. At that point, I really couldn't care less who contacted me because I was just relieved that whoever said today is my last chance would finally leave me alone. I filled in the form and ran out of the church as soon as I could. "No way am I coming back to this church again," I said to myself.

Watching porn was the only thing on my mind as soon as I got back home, especially after the whole drama that had occurred earlier in the church. As, I stepped indoors, I was overwhelmed by such a strong urge to watch porn. It was so enormous my entire body began to shake. The intensity, coupled with anxiety, was just so much that I had to watch porn and masturbate to help myself relax. While I was thinking about what type of movie to watch, I felt a sense of guilt come over me.

"This is strange," I said to myself. Never had it happened before since I started watching porn that I would feel guilty. *Something must be really wrong for me to be feeling guilty. Is it not the same porn I have been watching for more than ten years? Why then am I feeling guilty now?* I really could not place my thoughts on where the guilt about porn was coming from.

I then decided I was just going to ignore the guilt and watch porn regardless. Just as I inserted the DVD into the player, I heard what I had never heard before in my entire life. "Watching porn is not good". *What? Watching porn is not good. Who said that? Could I be talking to myself without knowing it? This isn't happening again. I must really be going crazy. I think I am. How could this be? Could it be the church that is doing this to me? But, there is no one here from church in my house! Who can then be telling me watching porn is not good?*

I had been told many times not to go anywhere near churches because nothing good comes out of it. I thought that had just been confirmed by my experience. I wondered whether it was the preacher's prayer that was causing me to be hearing these words. I wished he had not prayed the prayers.

In the midst of this confusing situation, I was also dealing with my body that would just not stop shaking. The anxiety was getting increasingly worse with each hour. *What is going on with me?* There I was trying to understand who it was that might be telling me watching porn isn't good and on the other hand I was trying to make my body relax. *What do I do now?* After about an hour pacing up and down my living room, I decided I was just going to watch it anyway. There is nobody here that could tell me watching porn isn't good.

As soon as I sat down to watch the porn movie the same words came back again, but this time around I ignored them. Just as I began to masturbate, for the first time in years I felt bad. This was different; this was not about me feeling bad it seemed someone was feeling bad for me. *This is strange.* I could just sense I wasn't the only one person in the house that day.

The next morning, "Watching porn is not good," was the first thought that flashed through my mind I opened my eyes. *I must truly be going crazy now. What is going on with me? Why am I having these thoughts? Could it be because of prayer I said in that church last night?* Throughout the week it seemed I was in a fight to satisfy my body and at the same time listen to the thoughts in my head telling me watching porn isn't good. But most importantly, I said to myself there was no way I was going to go back to the church ever again. *I am definitely staying away from that church. If anyone in that church ever calls me, I am going to cuss, and tell them never to call me again, and if they do I am definitely going to report them to the police.*

12

THE CRY FOR FREEDOM

Freedom cannot be defined or explained until you have been held in prison

What! Why am I even thinking of going to that church again? Did I not promise myself I would never step into that church or any church ever again? Why am I looking forward to going to the church, after what they have done to me?

It was the following Sunday and I was up and ready, heading towards the church that I had promised to never ever attend. Interestingly I knew that when the preacher is about to climb the stand, everyone stood. So, I was quick to stand up. Just as I was standing, the same thought at that Wednesday evening service when I prayed the preacher's prayer came back. Soon I began to feel guilty. "Watching porn is not good," just kept playing in my head. I looked around thinking it was the guy next to me but it wasn't. This guy was too focused. He wouldn't care less who I was. *I think there is a problem with this church.*

Back home I said to myself, "That is the end of that church. How can you pray a prayer and ever since then, it seems there is someone now following you about the entire town?"

It was finally summer time. I was looking out through my bedroom window. That year, summer had been beautiful but on this particular day there wasn't anything spectacular. Down below, I could see everyone having the best of times in the local park. I was thinking to myself that I might join them but that was a mere wish because my university final year exams were about two months away.

As usual the afternoon began to roll into evening and the sun drifted under the cloud slowly. It appeared I was living in a dark closed box with no way of escape. Since the day began, I had been battling with two thoughts. One thought was telling me that watching porn and masturbating was not good. Another thought was telling me to masturbate. *This isn't the first time you have found yourself in this same place. All it takes is just one hour of a porn movie and your body will relax.* My mind screamed, "Stop! Could you just shut up? I don't want to masturbate and I am not going to masturbate or watch porn."

That battle continued for about 3 hours. I hadn't left my room since I woke up but it seemed like I had just returned from a football match. My head felt so heavy. *I wish someone would just walk in and help me stop these thoughts. Who can help me choose which thoughts to go with?* Deep inside of me, I wanted to stop masturbating but the strength to say no wasn't just there. I felt the two thoughts battling for control of my will in a tug of war. Finally, I gave in! *Who cares if I watch porn or masturbate? I am going to die with this addiction. No one will be able to help me. Whatever is telling me to watch porn wins? I will do it. I will watch porn and masturbate and that will be the end of it.*

Like I usually would do whenever I wanted to watch porn, I put on my laptop to watch something that would curb my strong desire. I did a search on my regular sites; there weren't any hard-core porn on my usual sites. I felt the ones I was seeing were just too soft. After spending roughly two hours going through the entire library of movies, I finally found the one I believed will fuel my desire.

As usual the site was requesting for payment. I went through my wallet and got my bank card. "I think I still have some money left to get me through my exam session. Who cares I will manage like I always do," was the thought that went through my mind. Only God knows how much I must have spent this week on porn. *But now is not the time to be thinking or feeling sorry for myself. All I need is porn.*

I entered my card details and the movie was on. I thought it would be hard core. But it wasn't. I had seen it before but it was too late because all I really wanted to do was to watch, masturbate and get rid of the strong desire. Some minutes into the movie, the guilt came creeping in but I kept ignoring it while watching my porn. Throughout the time I was watching and masturbating, the guilt wouldn't just go away. As soon I finished watching the porn movie, it seemed a heavy shower of guilt rained upon me. It was the strongest I had ever felt; more than when I first attended the Church, this one was much heavier. It seemed there was someone standing next to me telling me watching porn is not good. Suddenly just like that I burst into tears. I was crying so heavily. I could not contain myself but cried and cried for about 10 minutes. Could someone help me? *Could someone please help me get rid of this masturbating? Look at my life! No money to even put food on my table. I don't even know how I am going to pass my exam. Is this what life is about? Could I ever be free from this addiction?* Out of desperation I shouted, "Father, take this thing away. I am tired of watching porn. I am really tried."

Just like that! It appears a light bulb went off inside of me. I stood up and wiped my face and blew my nose. I stared at my laptop for a while and before I knew what was going on I began to delete all the porn movies on my laptop. In order to ensure there wasn't anything left in an unnamed folder, I decided to reformat the entire laptop. I turned the laptop back on and went through the process again just to be doubly sure.

There was a surge of energy within me driving me to delete and reformat my laptop. I logged back into all my porn accounts and cancelled all my subscriptions. I went into my mail box and deleted every single password that unlocked the door to porn sites. I ensured every single email was deleted. Next I walked towards my bed where I had kept my collection of porn magazines and DVDs. I held the side of the mattress and raised it up and there they were. All the old and new collections of magazines and DVDs. I began to remove every single item. Within me I felt a sense of anger. How could someone be watching such kind of movies?

I headed towards the living room where a stack of porn DVDs was hidden under the chairs. Some were kept in the store room. Still angry, I got hold of a bin bag from the kitchen and started filling it up with porn DVDs and magazines. I ensured every item was ripped into pieces. I still could not understand all that was going on but coming back upstairs, I told myself I needed to get out of the house straight away. I had already discussed with Tom about staying at his place during my exam revision. Immediately, I was on the phone to Tom.

"Hello, Tom. It's Ty on the line. Can I come and spend some time with you? I need a place near university where I could study and sleep instead of travelling back to London each day." Everything tumbled out of my mouth in a desperate cry for help.

Tom hesitated for a while then said, "Why not, you can come along but you will have to contribute towards food shopping".

"That won't be a problem," I replied

"When will you like to come over?"

"Now?"

"Now"! Why the urgency?"

"Nothing," I replied trying to hide the desperation in my voice.

All this was happening so fast until I realised I had to make the biggest decision of my life. I had never left my laptop behind before; wherever I go, it goes it with me. *What do I do now? Should I go with it and trust myself not to visit porn sites? Decision... decision. What do I do now?*

I had to make a decision. Whatever decision I made would have a consequence because I didn't want to be watching porn in Tom's house. After going back and forth deliberating whether to take it or leave it behind, I decided I was going to take it but I would use Tom's laptop instead of mine if I needed to go on the internet.

What is going on with me? Why am I heading to Tom's house so quickly? I think I should go next day, but within me I felt a compelling surge of inner strength urging me to leave the house. I did not know what was directing my action but there I was heading to Tom's house where I was going to stay for the next three months also.

13

FIRST NIGHT WITHOUT PORN OR MASTURBATING

I began to get apprehensive; the thought of how I was going get through the night without masturbating was now getting to me. *How am I going to survive the night?*

I couldn't remember the last time I went to bed without masturbating. The last time was before I turned 12. I decided I wasn't going to let Tom know what had been going in my life. While Tom was showing me where everything was in the house, where things were kept, I just followed him around the house trying to concentrate on every word he spoke.

"Ty, this is where you will be sleeping."

"What"?

"Have you not been listening all this while"?

"Of course I have"

"I have got you a pump bed which you will be using during your time here".

"I replied 'No problem".

As the time for bed drew closer, I began to get very anxious. *What is going to happen to me tonight?* I looked at the possibility of watching porn but with Tom in the room that wasn't going to happen. What have I got myself into? I can't even masturbate if I tried to; Tom would see what I am doing as he is just a couple of inches from me. The toilet was not an option. I didn't want someone to come to the door and find it locked and even realise I have been there for hours. I wasn't ready to gamble.

Lying on the pump bed during the early hours of the night was the longest night I had ever experience. I couldn't do anything but just stare at the celling. By now Tom's had begun to snore. *I began to think maybe I could sneak into the living room to watch porn and masturbate but getting caught in a house that is not mine was too much of a risk.* I was pondering these thoughts when I fell asleep.

What! It's morning! Did it just happen? Did I just sleep without masturbating? I looked across to where Tom was sleeping. He was curled up under his duvet.

I stood up and ran to the toilet locked the door behind me and pulled down my trousers and my pants. What! My pant is dry! This isn't happening. Did I just sleep without masturbating? This can't be true. I could not control myself in the toilet; I was jumping for joy while the door was locked behind me. It was still very early in the morning and I was very cautious not to wake anybody up or draw any attention. I sat on the toilet full of joy. Did it just happen? Did I just sleep without masturbating?

On arriving at the library early in the morning, there wasn't anyone in the section where I went to sit, I dropped my bag and started pacing the entire library. I found it ex-

FIRST NIGHT WITHOUT PORN OR MASTURBATING

tremely difficult to sit still. I didn't know whether to run around the library with my hands held up high. If other students saw me, they might think someone was going crazy. I found it difficult to even concentrate on my revision throughout the day. The thought of not masturbating was so much to contain. I just sat down and stared at the beautiful Victorian drawing on the ceiling.

I cannot believe it is truly happening! Is this really possible? Can it actually be true? Back at home after the little revision I was able to get through in the library, with my back on the bed, and staring at the ceiling. Can it really be true? I was about to go to bed and for the first time in years there are no thoughts or desire to watch porn before sleeping. No strong desire whatsoever to masturbate.

Normally, each time I tried closing my eyes to sleep, I could see pictures of ladies from porn movies and magazines and the ones I fantasized about. Shutting my eyes was the last thing I wanted to do because of these pictures. Now there I was, my eyes shut and those images of ladies that I usually saw have finally disappeared. There were no pictures whatsoever. Wow!

The pain that was constantly around my lower abdomen and my penis had stopped and the swelling around my privates seemed to have disappeared. The everyday headache and anxiety had totally disappeared. The constant fear of something bad happening to me had also left.

The regular thoughts pushing me to harm myself had finally stopped. "Jump and kill yourself, No way are you ever going to be free. Just end your life. You are never going be free. You are going to die masturbating and watching porn all through the rest of your life. You can never stop sleeping with prostitutes. If your friend and family found out who you are and what you do, they will make fun of you. End your life before you become a laughing matter."

What I was experiencing at that moment was an indescribable and unexplainable peace. Peace that is difficult to describe but at the same time very present around and within me. It seemed I was enveloped in peace. Where can it be coming from? What is going on with me lately?

I believed meeting the man they call Jesus is the reason for all this. The heavy condemnation that always followed me about no longer follows me. I can feel and touch freedom. Wow! I can so much taste freedom it seems I am floating in the air.

Why will this Jesus do what he did? I had heard so much about this Jesus while growing. I was told he is a very bad man and he punishes everyone that breaks his law. But, since I met Jesus on that Wednesday evening he hasn't done any bad thing to me, only good things.

I even heard that all this Jesus wants is your money but I haven't paid him anything yet. Why will he then do what he did for me without asking for a penny in return? This must be crazy.

With all the porn movies I have watched, number of prostitutes I have slept with and the number of ladies I have masturbated to, I should be the last person he should be kind to. I think I need to know more about this Jesus the preacher that church is talking about.

14

WILL I SURVIVE?

Can I go back? What will happen if I go back? Am I ready for my old environment? Am I tough enough to cope by myself? What do I do now? While thinking on those thoughts Tom walked into the room.

"Ty, can we talk please?"

"Hope everything is okay?"

"Yes, everything is cool. I just wanted you know we will soon be returning the house back to the landlord."

"Soon, I did not know it was going to be that soon?" I was frantically trying to gather my thoughts so that I wouldn't say anything stupid. "Okay. No problem, I will get back to you by the end of the week to let you know when I plan to move back home."

What is going to happen to me now? Should I explain to Tom what has been happening in my life? Will that change anything? I don't think it would. Tom is such a good friend and I am sure he wouldn't have said so if the landlord hasn't requested the house back.

From that day, I became anxious about what would

happen if I returned to my old environment. *Do I think I have got what it takes to stay away from porn by myself?* I didn't think so.

The day I was to leave arrived too early. I was so disgruntled while I was packing my cloths and toiletries. By midday, I was ready to leave. I ensured Tom did not for once know what was rumbling within me and how unhappy I was to be leaving.

As I was approaching my home, I felt a deep sense of fear clouding over me. I looked at the staircase and it seemed as if I should just unpack and live on the staircase. As I opened the door to my flat, old memories of porn movies were just flooding back. I looked around and I noticed that my brother hadn't been home for a while.

I headed towards my room to drop my baggage. Just as soon I stepped in, I could see a picture of what I would usually do when I masturbated. *This cannot be happening so soon!*

I sat down at the edge of the bed with my hands resting on my lap thinking about what to do. *Should I rent a new house to get away from these horrible memories?* As I was thinking something caught my attention. *"What?" I exclaimed. How did I miss this one? I thought I collected everything from the house that day.*

Just there within a pile of books on the floor next to the bed was a porn DVD which I had missed when clearing out last time. I took it and held it in my hand. It was a tug of war. I debated over whether to keep it or destroy it. Something within me said, "You know you haven't watched porn for a long time." My thoughts were swinging back and forth between two camps: one camp said there is nothing bad if I watched it just this once; another said, "Break it now!"

I told myself that truly it's been a while since I last watched a porn movie. Watching it just this once won't cause me any harm. Would it? Just as I was about to settle on keeping it, a picture of all the struggles I have had with trying to stop masturbating just came flooding into my mind. The picture was so real I stood and said, "No!" As I was breaking the DVD, I stood up. Just like it happened the day I said, "Father please take this thing away", a strange feeling came on me. Immediately, giving it no extra thought, I ransacked the entire house starting with the book lying next to my bed.

I began to open each page one by one to ensure nothing was left. My next port of call was the attic. As soon as I opened the door to the attic, there they were staring directly at me, a huge collection of porn DVDs that I had forgotten even existed. "What!" I exclaimed. With everything I was wearing, my shirt and trousers. I jumped into the attic. I just could not believe what I was seeing. Porn DVDs were everywhere. I ransacked through some bin bags and I could see loads of magazines. *How did I miss these ones?*

I was fuming. With all the rage within me, I began to tear up magazines and wildly stamp on every DVD. At the same time I began to say, "No way am I going back. No way!" Coming out from the attic, I was drenched in sweat like someone that has just completed a marathon.

Next port of call was the kitchen store. Wow! DVDs everywhere just like in the attic. Again, I madly smashed every single one of them. By then my entire house was upside down. Anyone that entered would have thought it had been ransacked by thieves.

It wasn't long after my bout of marathon clearing when I settled down to relax that an overwhelming desire to watch porn flooded my mind. What is going on? I stood up to engage in some house cleaning to see if the thoughts would leave but the thoughts wouldn't just go away. I began to get worried and wondered what I could do to stop the constant deluge of filthy thoughts. To make matters worse, my body also began to respond in a strange away and it seemed as if my physical body was saying, "Hey! I need to have sex. You have been starving me of sex for two months." I said "this cannot be happening!" Sex was the last thing on my mind and there I was fighting the temptation to go to Soho for sex.

I had only just been back from Tom's house and it seemed I was in the middle of two raging battles. One was with the constant flow of thoughts that kept telling me I needed to masturbate in order to relax, and the other with my physical body that kept demanding for sex. Who can I run to now for help? My brother hadn't a clue what had been going on lately. Not knowing what to do, without thinking about at it I began to say, "Jesus help me! Jesus help me!" It seemed all the thoughts just stopped immediately. How it happened, I can't tell.

As night time approached, I began to get anxious. This was the first night I would be spending in the very house where every night I routinely watched porn then masturbated before going to bed. Not only that, I started having flashbacks of what I used do on the bed before I sleep. I decided I wasn't going to sleep on the bed but use the living room instead. It didn't work. That also brought flashbacks of where I would normally sit whenever I am watching porn and what I would normally do. It just seemed that the entire house, every single room was turning against me.

I even contemplated sleeping in the corridor between the living room and the bedroom. But, then the thoughts of what I would usually do in the toilets evaded my mind. I stood for a while leaning on the door frame of the room looking outside through the window. My mind travelled back to the very first day I watched a porn DVD and how happy I was. I remembered how I began to collect and buy DVDs thinking it was the coolest thing to do then. Fast forward from that time to today, I wish I was never introduced to it. I regretted the day I met G who introduced me to porn. By the time I realised it, it was close to midnight. By then, I felt so exhausted and all I could remember was walking straight towards my bed and throwing myself on it.

Waking up the next day, not long after I opened my eyes, the thoughts of watching porn just came flooding into my mind, and my physical body began to demand sex just like it did the day before.

Just like the previous day, I knew when I said, "Jesus, please help!" All the thoughts stopped. So I began to say, "Jesus help! Jesus help!" The thoughts stopped and my body was back to normal again. Throughout the day whenever the thoughts of watching porn came back to me

I kept saying "Jesus help!" I said to myself, "I think this man called Jesus is really working."

In the following days, things took a turn for the worse. Each time I woke up in the morning or even after an afternoon nap, my body would discharge semen. Sometimes I had to wake up more than three times to clean myself. Falling asleep became scary. I couldn't understand it at first.

One particular day, I woke up and it dawned on me what had been happening while I was fast asleep. Like a movie my mind was playing back the pictures I used to imagine myself masturbating with various women. Even though I was asleep, my body was responding to what was going on in my mind without my physical involvement.

That day, my pants were totally soaked in semen. I sat on the edge of my bed and I began to cry profusely asking what was wrong me. I began to say, "Jesus, I thought you have freed me from this porn. Why is this happening to me?" I cried until I had no more strength left to cry. I was just greatly disappointed and felt helpless.

By then, I had been attending church regularly and getting to know more about Jesus. I had come to know he died for my sins so that I could be free. Notwithstanding, the temptation to watch porn and have sex was still so strong.

While sitting on the edge of my bed, I thought to myself that if no one had the answer to whatever is happening to me, then the preacher of the church I was attending should. I decided to call the preacher and explain what had been going on and how I had been freed from porn and masturbating for two months. I told him how since arriving back from university, I had struggled with a strong temptation to watch porn and have sex. I couldn't bring myself to tell the preacher that I had sex with prostitutes too.

The preacher took a deep pause and said, "Son, do not worry. Remember the devil does not want you to be free. That is the reason why he is throwing everything at you. Just make sure you don't go back to watching porn and masturbating. Son don't give up; stand your ground. Jesus has already freed you and the battle will soon be over." He asked if I had the bible on CD or if I could download it to my mp3 player. He told me to play it everyday, ensuring it was playing at all times.

Days then turned into weeks and weeks into months and at first, it seemed the discharge of semen would not stop. However, as I followed the preacher's advice to play the bible in my room and on my mp3, the semen discharge began to reside.

He also advised me to start attending church. Not long after I began to attend church regularly, I noticed clarity in my thought process for the first time in years. Clarity of thought is something I had been struggling with for years and at last I was regaining my ability to think about what will happen in the following hours. Before then, I would struggle to imagine anything because each time I tried to, it seemed all I could see were pictures of women. Each day began to seem like a step forward.

At last, I had money to spend on anything I desired. I was able to eat good food instead of wasting money on internet porn, porn movies or sleeping with prostitutes.

15

WILL I EVER GET MARRIED?

I have sailed through seven years without a relapse. But those years were a tough struggle. At first, it looked as if I could never be totally free. Each day I felt like I was taking a giant step. Every hour was a battle. It seemed I would never be able to use my brain for anything else ever again. Reasoning was a challenge. Thinking about masturbating and porn was all I had been used to for many years. Concentrating on a task seemed so difficult. It just felt like my brain wandered about every second of the day and keeping it focused on anything in particular was a huge challenge.

Over time, true freedom started becoming real. I was able to go to bed without having to masturbate or watch porn. My body was not demanding sex like it used to. I felt my body responding quite well to the Bible CD I'd been listening to. If someone had said to me that I would be able to go through the streets of Soho without knocking on any prostitute's door, I would have called that person a liar. But, there I was one day walking around Soho town and there was no desire whatsoever to go into a sex shop or strip bar.

Coming from work on another day, I realised I had walked past a sex shop every single day without noticing. That day, I stood and looked at a display window and I breathed a huge sigh of relief. These shops and many others were my home for over 14 years. But, there I was looking at the shop and there wasn't any desire, not even a single thought, to go into the store and check what they were doing inside. This Jesus is special! Those strong desires that always propelled me to go into those places have now disappeared completely.

Jesus also restored my entire brain faculties – the ability to think, the ability to imagine my future. The fear and worry that used to follow me about every day and controlled me has now been replaced with peace, undeniable peace that cannot be described; the sort of peace that when people see you, they clearly notice it in you.

At one of our regular catch-ups one day, my mentor asked, "Son when are you getting married?"

"Sir, I don't see myself getting married with what I have been through sexually in life."

He looked straight at me with a smile on his face and said, "Son, marriage to a woman will bring total wholeness for you. Never close your mind to getting married. The right woman will complete you."

At that moment in his office I was thinking there was no chance I was going to get married but he was right. Today, like he said I am happily married and supported by a wonderful lady that loves me for who I am and the transformation Jesus has made in my life. You could probably be thinking it impossible for a man that was addicted to porn, masturbation, and sleeping with prostitutes to ever get married. By myself, it would never have been possible. But there is someone who specialises in restoring lost years and broken lives. His name is Jesus!

Will I say I have not been tempted along the way? Many times the temptation has come but I have always remembered to depend on Jesus and cry to him to help me each time. He has not for once in the last seven years left me without coming to my support.

I believe Jesus has been kind to me more than anyone in this world. His unconditional love has filled my life to the overflow.

16

CONGRATULATIONS! YOU MADE IT

If you have taken time to read this book, I would like to congratulate you for coming this far. I strongly believe my story has either impacted you or given you a different perspective on the dangers of porn and masturbating.

There are many people today that would say there isn't anything wrong with watching porn. They might even say masturbating is good. Media and society have made us believe that watching porn simply spices up our sex lives, helping couples have a better sex life. But, reading my story you would have realised that that is not the case.

My view based on my experience is that porn looks beautiful from the outside with its beautiful enticing images of women; but, it's actually a deadly virus that destroys the lives of its victims gradually. I am telling my story to let you see the devastating effects that porn can have on someone's life and then leave you to make your own choice. But, if I were you, I would quit before it takes over my life.

If you are a teenager reading this book right now, I believe this is the best book you would have read about the impact of porn on the life of an individual. As a young boy growing up, I succumbed to the daily pressure from friends in school and to my own curiosity. Just because I wanted to fit in with my friends and really didn't want to be left out, I joined them in watching what I should not have been watching in the first place. Watching porn seemed like I was having the best time of my life. But, things began to spiral out of hand, first into masturbation at the tender age of 12 and by 20, I was a porn junkie. I was masturbating every day and everywhere you can imagine. There wasn't anywhere I couldn't masturbate. It was that bad: public toilets, college toilets, anywhere. As a young boy, I did not know any better. I just thought I was having fun. I didn't know there was going to be a huge consequence for what I was doing.

Remember your friends will always tell you there is nothing wrong with porn. They may even laugh at you if you don't know what it is about. I'd like you to remember that the consequence of watching it would not show straightaway; over time it will creep into your personal life like it did into mine and take over your mind, spirit and body. My advice for you is to stop before it destroys your brain. If you're already struggling with porn, I want to tell you, you can become totally free.

To the man – husband, father and anyone out there reading this book, if you are struggling with porn, I have got good news for you: there is hope for you and you too can become totally free no matter how bad your addiction is.

17

YOU CAN BE FREE

I mean it. You can be free from addiction to pornography and all the other filth that comes with it. You have seen from my story, how I had totally destroyed the brain God gave me. He gave me a body which he had described as his 'temple' in the bible (1 Corinthians 6:19), and I misused it. It doesn't matter how messed up you are, God can free you from your addiction. He has every reason to. Hear this:

> Do you not know that your bodies are members of Christ? Shall I then take the members of Christ and make them members of a prostitute? Never! Or do you not know that he who is joined to a prostitute becomes one body with her? For, as it is written, "The two will become one flesh." But he who is joined to the Lord becomes one spirit with him. Flee from sexual immorality. Every other sin a person commits is outside the body, but the sexually immoral person sins against his own body. Or do you

not know that your body is a temple of the Holy Spirit within you, whom you have from God? You are not your own, for you were bought with a price. So glorify God in your body.

1 Corinthians chapter 6, verses 15 – 20, English Standard Version

God loves you. He calls you precious, loved, chosen. He wants to restore you. Porn addicts aren't the only ones that are messed up; the whole world was blighted by the debilitating effects of sin. So, long before I was born, long before you were born, God made a way for each of us to become free from all forms of sin. His way of rescuing us from sin and its consequences was to give us Jesus.

From my story, you'd remember that I had to accept that I was an addict and a sinner before God and ask Jesus for forgiveness and help. That is the way out.

"But, what about sex therapists, counsellors and other forms of help?" you may ask. I really do not have any problem with sex therapists or counsellors. One thing they can't guarantee is your total freedom forever. There is someone who can give you the freedom you desire. You don't even have to pay him anything. And, that person is Jesus. Since I accepted Jesus into my life, my life has never been the same. I'm totally free from the addiction that was going to ruin my future.

Jesus came to the earth to save us for sin and to ensure that we can life to the fullest (John 10:10), just as God intended for each and every man and woman. Sin offends God. But, Jesus took the punishment you deserved by dying on a cross, and carrying all your sin upon himself. He did this so that when you ask God to, he would pardon you for your sin. Jesus didn't just die but he rose up from the grave so that you and I would truly be free from the 'grave' of sin including addiction to pornography.

He could have left us to carry those addictions for the rest of our lives without any help. But, he looked at us and our suffering and decided we are too precious to be left helpless and lost to sin. God really loved everyone in the world and he sent Jesus, so that anyone that believes in him would not perish but have everlasting life (John 3:16).

So, I implore you to ask Jesus to forgive you and to come into your life and turn it around. It is an important decision you need to make in order to experience the freedom I now have.

If you have made that decision to walk away from porn and masturbating to experience true freedom, I want you to say the simple prayer below with sincerity. It's the same sort of prayer I prayed that invited Jesus into my life and began the restoration process. I'm confident it will work for you too.

> "Heavenly Father, I come to you in the name of Jesus. I realise I am a sinner and that Jesus died for me so that I can be free from sin including my addiction. So, I ask you to forgive me for all I have done wrong. I ask Jesus to come into my heart right now and be Lord over my life. Thank you Father. I am now a born again Christian."

If you have prayed this prayer I congratulate you. You may be wondering, "Elisha is that all I have to do?" Yes, it is for you to start living free. Find a bible-believing church where you can be supported as you live a new life in Jesus. Also, visit my website www.elishakolade.org for useful information and resources to help you.

Finally I would like to welcome you to your hour of freedom I am waiting to hear your testimony. Welcome to the life of freedom and peace. Jesus is Lord!

COMING SOON

Pathway to FREEDOM
THE STORY OF A PORN ADDICT

ELISHA KOLADE

Lightning Source UK Ltd.
Milton Keynes UK
UKOW06f2044280815

257740UK00002B/6/P